Tawanda Forever

A journey of bravery and resilience through cancer

TAWANDA CHAMUNORWA

Hey Sadru! thank you for being such a good friend and being so supportive.

Tawanda. C

RMPublishers Ltd, Kemp House 160 City Road, London
EC1V 2NX UNITED KINGDOM

As long as you are alive, you have a purpose to fulfil.

Tawanda Chamunorwa

Contents

Foreword

Mr Bassel Zebian - BSc (Hons), MBBS, MRCS (Engl) FRCS (Neuro. Surg)

I write this whilst waiting for Tawanda's most recent scan to appear on our imaging system at King's College Hospital. There is undoubtedly the prospect of further surgery. Tawanda and I discussed this over the phone along with his book, his label "Rare and Loved," and his overall commendable outlook on life.

I have known Tawanda for over seven years now. I first met him in 2014, shortly after taking my consultant post. He was unwell with a large tumour deep in his brain, causing brainstem dysfunction.

I vividly remember our first meeting. We discussed the benefits of surgery, the alternatives and the risks. We spoke about the chances of poor coordination and weakness in Tawanda's arms and legs and facial muscles, of problems with swallowing and breathing due to the tumour or surgery to remove the tumour. We discussed the risk to his life from the tumour, from surgery and residual tumour, should there be any.

Unfortunately, it's a relatively well-rehearsed speech – brain tumours are the most common solid tumours in children. Well-rehearsed, yet ever so difficult. With every word, the impact on patients and their families is palpable. It's as if their lives are turned upside down and destroyed, then rebuilt in one conversation. I have been on both sides of the fence, and despite years of doing it, it does not get any easier, nor do I expect it to. Nor, for that matter, should it get easier. The day we find such conversations easy is perhaps the day we have lost our humanity.

The courage that fellow human beings display in their darkest hours never ceases to amaze me. This courage drives them through and out of that darkness – whether their tumour is benign or malignant, curable, controllable or far advanced. Tawanda was diagnosed at an age where its impact was hardest felt. Yet, incomplete insight gives a degree of resilience to the very young. With advancing age, life equips us with coping strategies in the face of adversity. When such adversity hits us in our teenage years, these strategies can be lacking or underdeveloped, but the calibre of the problem is not lost on us.

Tawanda displayed a great deal of courage from the outset. He had unwavering support from his mother – often, the most difficult conversations were had with her first. They both had a great deal of faith which helped them along the journey. They were also surrounded by many relatives and friends who all rallied to offer support. Nonetheless, I know that Tawanda would have at times felt utterly alone. We benefit most from talking to those in a similar situation, especially if they went through the same obstacles ahead of us. We usually fear the unknown.

Support groups go a long way in revealing that unknown, and I am confident that this book will play its part in being a friend to those who are going through a similar journey to Tawanda. It is not exhaustive – Tawanda's journey is far from over. It is, however, genuine, true and pure. Tawanda demonstrated that throughout a difficult initial period, recurrence and the need for further treatment, he was and still is able and eager to continue living his life to its fullest. I would like to express my most sincere gratitude to Tawanda and his family for allowing me the privilege to care for him and support him and for sharing his story. He is indeed "Rare and Loved."

Karen Powell, CNS Nurse, RGN, RN Child (dip BSC (Children

The name "Tawanda Chamunorwa" was first heard in our weekly meeting with the Neurosurgeons, Radiologists and Oncology team, where we discuss new patients diagnosed with brain or spinal tumours. For weeks, we heard about this young man in Intensive care; we saw his scans and examined his brain and his tumour millimetre by millimetre by millimetre. We saw his facial profile on the scan and heard about his progress out of ITU until he started treatment. We didn't know Tawanda, though - that came with years of treatment, follow up calls and meetings because he is much more than his diagnosis. So many setbacks and side effects are all borne with stoic, quiet determination. Even the most challenging discussions take place with calm resilience.

Nobody should be defined by their diagnosis, but for some, you see them grow and exceed all expectations physically and emotionally, turning something negative into a positive and using it for good. We often say that looking after our patients, and walking alongside them is a privilege, and it seems so cliche and cheesy. Still, to get to know them -to be welcomed into their life, family and community is the most precious experience.

Tawanda has held strong, and whilst he may not realise or appreciate it fully, we know that he has positively affected other young people undergoing treatment who have met him, and his strength has been passed on. There are days when caring for patients is hard - emotionally exhausting, and you can get worn down by the sadness of witnessing what young people are going through. But the magic they have within, the love and care they and their families give back, makes it bearable and keeps the hope alive within us too.

Tawanda is rare and is loved by those that have been honoured to care for him.

* * *

Pastor Mel Kabaso BA (Hons Statistics, BA Social Work, MA Theology, Dip Business Studies

All of us have our heroes. My hero is Tawanda, and his life tells a story. I see many remarkable things in the life of Tawanda. One thing that moves me is Tawanda's unwavering faith amid calamities. Tawanda's first operation left him weakened and very ill. As a result of the first operation, he lost his body coordination and could not swallow food. Tawanda was living a shadow of life. He was walking through the valley of the shadow of death. Yet, living in the shadow of his life and walking in the valley of the shadow of death did not stop him from believing in God. Like David. **Psalm 23:4.** Tawanda is our psalmist who has walked in the valley of the shadow of death and has shown us that there is no shadow without light. His walk points to the ever-present light of God during the darkest moments of our lives.

Out of Tawanda's experience, I have a story to tell and a sermon to preach. Hebrews Chapter 11 is sometimes called the "Hall of Faith" as it reveals incredible ordinary men and women whose stories encourage and challenge our faith. They are also called the heroes of faith. Tawanda's story also makes it into the hall of faith, and he is my hero of faith.

He is a role model of our times, an ordinary young man who continues to trust God radically. I have leant some lessons from Tawanda's life:

- He has taught me that when your trial is severe and unbearable;
- when your pain and discomfort are so excruciating that you cannot sleep,
- that when you run out of ideas and the doctors cannot guarantee healing,

- that when the faces on people tell you things are bad,
- Tawanda has taught me to count it all joy and continue to look to God for an answer.

Tawanda has taught me that this is the best place to be when you don't know what to do. It allows you to depend on God totally. The preacher and teacher, Andrew Murray, called it *"Absolute Surrender".*

Tawanda has also taught me that you cannot know God just by what he has created, **Romans 1:20,** but also by his open door of grace. His grace is sufficient when you have a thorn in your flesh. Tawanda has had a thorn in his flesh for a long time. He has asked God to remove it, and God has pointed him to the door of grace- *my grace is sufficient.*

Tawanda, you are my hero of faith. A living testimony. Therefore, I am confident that this book will be a blessing to anyone who reads it.

Preface

In the Autumn of 2014, I was set to begin a new and exciting chapter in my life. I was young and ready to go off to University; little did I know that my life was about to change in a way that I or anyone around me could never have seen coming.

My name is Tawanda, and at the age of eighteen, I was diagnosed with a rare brain tumour, Ependymoma. My bags were packed, student accommodation booked, and I was all set to start the adventure of a lifetime. In two weeks' time, I would be off to University.

This diagnosis changed everything.

Cancer can change your life forever. Nobody ever thinks they will get it, I didn't, and it was the farthest thing from my mind at eighteen. So you would have thought that if I were to have cancer, I would at least have something easy to deal with, but no, the type of cancer that invaded my body was rare. Ependymomas are a type of brain tumour formed from the ependymal cells, the brain cells that produce cerebrospinal fluid (CSF). You may sometimes hear them referred to as glioma. (Brain Tumour Charity) This type of brain tumour is most common in children.

The fight for my life began in 2014, and it has been a long and challenging journey. We still have no idea when the Ependymomas may have started growing in my body. I have had some good and bad days where my life was hanging on the line. There were days I felt like an overcomer - like I can do this, I can fight this! Yet, on some, I found myself struggling with depression and ready to give up on life. But I have kept going and fighting. The little reminders from family and friends that my life still had a purpose and that they loved me kept me going.

This book narrates my story. I not only share my journey as I fight for my life; I share my pain, struggles, my wins and how I kept going. The diagnosis and everything else I have gone through has set me apart. I am also aware that many others worldwide have similar or worse battles than mine; I want them to know that they are not alone.

Out of my experiences, I created a brand called *Rare and Loved*. It is for extraordinary individuals who have rare health conditions or life-altering experiences that set them apart. It is a safe platform and home for RARE and LOVED fighters! This is my way of giving back and showing my gratitude for the gift of life.

I hope to inspire and encourage someone through my story.

Posing with my awards and trophies for various achievements

Acknowledgements

I want to thank my family and friends for standing with me throughout my life and cancer journey. I could write another book to thank the community and the many people who have been there with me.

To my mum, Maina Chamunorwa, you never left my bedside; we have been through all the ups and downs together. You are my real-life heroine and the actual definition of a strong woman. You have seen it all, but you continue to fight this battle with me. You are my Commander in Chief, constantly defending and protecting me.

My angel, in the form of a little sister, Tyah Chamunorwa, I am so sorry that you've had to grow so fast; I am proud of the young woman you have become. You are my joy and thank you for bringing laughter into our home, even in the most challenging moments. I love your baking, @tyahsbakes, and I know you will one day be the best baker in the whole world.

My favourite uncle, Anthony Chamunorwa, his beautiful wife, Rhodah Chamunorwa and their family. Thank you for always showing love. Aunty Rhodah, keep the food coming. I will never forget and appreciate your delicious food parcels. You two are our pillars and thank you for bringing unity to our family.

My aunty Cynthia Masiyiwa Mukoko and uncle Tawanda Mukoko, are my very own informal managers and advisors. You have helped me grow, and are always there to support me with my ventures. I value the time you take to support me and offer professional help. It is comforting to know that I have people like you who want to see me succeed.

Thank you to Teenage Cancer Trust, Macmillan Cancer Support, Teens Unite, Clic Sargent, The Royal Marsden charity, Brain tumour charity, Ray of sunshine, Black women Rising, Trekstock, etc. Your support has been tremendous. You have inspired me in so many ways, and I am a firm believer in your work because it has significantly impacted me.

Liz Hudson, Clic Sargent social worker, I cannot list everything you have done for my family and me, but every achievement in my life was because of you. You helped me remove any barriers that were in my way. You cheered me on even when I wanted to give up, and you picked up the phone every time I needed someone to talk to. You opened doors of opportunities for me and connected me with so many destiny helpers. You are a rare gem, and I sincerely appreciate you.

I have always appreciated the National Health Service (NHS), but I appreciate it even more since being a regular patient for more than seven years. So many wonderful people have made my journey comfortable and cared for me. Special mention to my surgeon, Dr Zebian & his team from King's College Hospital, Oncologist Consultant Dr Henry Mandeville, Specialist Clinical Nurse Karen Powell and the team at Royal Marsden Hospital. Sincere thanks to the health care professionals from every hospital that has cared for me.

When I started this journey, I was an Awake Grace Ministries member, led by an amazing couple, Pastors Mr and Mrs Kabaso. These Pastors, their leadership team and the extended church family have been my absolute rocks. The church is about community and love. Thank you for showing up always and for showing me, love. I now go to Hillsong Church. Special mention also goes to my connect group leaders and friends Sayo Ogundayo, Bukky Brown, Gabriel Brown, Sayo Dockers and Lewis Dockery and everyone from Hillsong Church. Pastor Given Mazarura from Awake Grace Ministries is not a lawyer; still, he has fought many legal battles on my behalf with Bukky and Gabriel Brown. Fighting to protect my business and everything that I believe in.

University of Kent (Medway). Thank you to Sarah Dening (mentor), Sian Newman (study skills mentor), Dr Kyra De Coninck, Dr Steve Meadows, Mr Karthikeyan Muthumayandi, all lecturers and staff. You helped me cross over and achieve my most significant achievement to date. It took a village of staff who cared so much to carry me, push me and empower me. I will forever be grateful. Best university in the whole world!

Last but not least, to the two amazing women who have made this book happen, my very own dream midwife Vonayi Nyamazana and the Queen of Comms, Victoria Chareka. I always pray that God sends me helpers, and you both are an answer to my prayer. This book would not have happened without your hard work and commitment. I had this dream for a long time, and I was far from achieving it, but you came into my life, and within a few months, you showed me what was possible. You believed in me, and you looked beyond my insecurities and fears and pushed me into greatness.

Above all, I thank God for walking with me throughout this journey. When I had nothing, my faith remained.

RIP to my father, Teddy Zvomuya. My first hero. I miss you, and I dedicate this book to you. Fly high!

With my father. Teddy Zvomuya. South Africa 1998

1

We Never Saw It Coming

With my mother, Maina Chamunorwa

I love football, and I was always outside, playing with my friends. I realised that something was not right when I started experiencing symptoms that made it hard to play outside with my friends. I was not feeling well. No one thought much of these symptoms, but looking back now, they were the first signs that something was wrong. I didn't think that the dizziness, the loss of balance and blurred vision, could be anything major. No one did.

In the beginning, I was only getting a few mild symptoms here and there. At first, the General Practitioner (GP) thought that I might have an ear infection, so he prescribed antibiotics. I took them and thought that the symptoms would disappear and I would be okay. And sure enough, the symptoms would go, but maybe for two or so months and then reappear. As time went on, the symptoms got worse and more frequent. Every time I went back to see the GP, he would prescribe even more antibiotics.

At one point, the GP thought that my eyes could be causing the problems because of the loss of balance and headaches. So I went off to get my eyes checked and got prescribed a pair of glasses, and we all thought that was the end of that. I wore the glasses for a while but soon realised that they didn't fix the problem.

This see-saw with the GP went on for two years, and it was clear that my health was deteriorating. The symptoms got worse. I had to cope with migraines, loss of balance, dizziness, blurred vision and fatigue almost daily. By this time, I could not engage in many physical activities. I stopped going out because of fear of falling and being run over by cars, especially when my vision and balance became bad. I missed a lot of school because of all that was happening to me.

I was confused because the doctors did not know why I was so unwell. But **IF** - if from the very start, the doctors had taken me seriously and referred me for a Magnetic Resonance Imaging (MRI) scan, maybe all this merry-go-round, which went on for about two years, would not have happened. Maybe I could have been diagnosed a lot sooner? So many maybes - I will never know.

Enough is enough!

Eventually, my mum got really angry and put her foot down. She demanded that I have further investigations done, and initially, they did blood tests to see if they could find anything. I waited about two weeks before we got the results back - they hadn't found anything in my blood. I went back to the GP; my mum was distraught and frustrated because she could see me deteriorating every day, yet nobody could tell us why. The whole situation was too frustrating.

Finally, the Ear, Nose and Throat department (ENT) referred me for an MRI scan, and I must have waited two weeks to have the scan. It was then that everything changed. We went to Lewisham Hospital for the MRI scan, and my mum began to suspect that things were not okay because it took so long for them to get back to us. I went in for the scan at 1 pm, and it took four hours for them to get back to us with the results. They said there was a shadow on my brain (I guess they did not want to scare my mum and me at that point). The Consultants explained that they wanted to send the scan to the neuro specialists for further investigations. So we had another three hours of investigations that took us into the evening; it may have been 7 pm by then.

Eventually, someone advised us that I had a tumour on my brain and needed an emergency operation. I was admitted straight away for surgery the next day if I gave my consent. They were transferring me to Kings College Hospital for the operation in the morning. My mum left, and I stayed overnight.

After mum left, everything started to sink in. My faith in God helped me at that time. I listened to different motivational messages and music that kept me positive. But on that crucial night, I didn't have too many thoughts and soon fell asleep. The hospital staff woke me up at 4 am to go to Kings College. It was quieter then, and I remember that one of the medics, who transferred me from Lewisham hospital to Kings College, was very nice. He said some kind words to me.

Everything started to move very fast then.

2

It was all happening – at last!

The symptoms were relentless. The following day I was to be nil by mouth. I was transferred to King's College Hospital early in the morning, around 5 am. I managed to get some sleep before mum and her friend arrived, and after that, the doctors came and explained everything to us. The tumour was 5.5 cm and pressing on my brain. After further deliberations, the Consultants decided not to operate that morning but put me on steroids for seven days to shrink the tumour before they operated.

I could hear the Consultants talking to me, but I don't think I was taking anything in. It was going in one ear and coming out the other—nothing sunk in. I just wanted them to get on and do whatever it took to get rid of the symptoms which were messing up my life. But, of course, by then, I had a whole load of symptoms; dizziness, loss of balance, vomiting, migraines, double and bloody vision.

I also remember that at one point, I started hearing voices. I think that it was a result of the pressure on the brain. The voices were so loud and real that I rushed to mum's room, crying with my hands over my ears. I wanted the voices to stop; it was a terrifying experience. Fatigue was a major symptom; I was always tired; my body was getting weaker and weaker. I think my puberty was interrupted at this time because of everything that was taking place. I started puberty late and soon after became very sick.

I'm not sure what was going on in my mind, but I could see that people around me were very concerned for me. On the other hand, they were all very nice to me; I could sense from the nurses that what I was about to go through was not minor. I don't think we were fully aware of the risks and complications involved despite the Consultants' explanation. The Consultants had told us that there was a risk of memory loss and paralysis and that I could go into a coma, among many others. I had seven days of steroids; they made me feel hungry, and I found myself eating anything I could get my hands on.

I told one of my friends, Jelisa, that I was in the hospital waiting to have surgery, and she surprised me the next day by coming to visit. A lot of my family members also came to visit me. I was in a ward, and only three people were allowed in at a time, but there was a waiting room where everyone could gather and wait. I still had the symptoms, but they weren't as bad, and I guess this was because of the steroids. I had dizziness, which slowed my movements down. As the days went by, it hit me that I would have a big operation. I was starting to get scared while trying to stay positive, but yeah...I was scared. As we got closer to the day of the surgery, I began to think that maybe I was going to die.

The seven days are up

We got to Friday, and my seven days on steroids were up. They had put me on *nil by mouth* from midday till the following morning when they were to operate. My family arrived at around 7 am; uncles, aunts and pastors. My family accompanied me to the theatre doors, and the doctors reassured me that all would be well. My aunty, Pastor Mavis, asked if she could pray for the surgeon, and before he could answer, she took his hands and prayed for him to have wisdom from above as he operated. The operation started at 9 am. A family friend who works at the hospital bought food from a nearby Morrison's to feed everyone waiting outside.

The Consultants and I went through the form so that I would know the risks involved and give my consent to the surgery. After signing the form, the theatre staff wheeled me in for surgery. The operation should have taken seven to eight hours, but it took double that time - fourteen hours. The tumour was big, and it was located in the posterior foss, making it difficult for the surgeons to remove. The fact that I had been poorly before the surgery complicated the situation. My family waited the whole fourteen hours while I was in surgery.

Mum, have you had breakfast yet?

All my family and friends were anxious because I didn't come out of surgery at the expected time and thought that something terrible had happened. They were worried, not knowing what was happening, but they continued praying until I came out fourteen hours later. It was 1 am the next day when I came out and was taken to the High Dependency Unit (HDU). After the surgery, I could talk even though I was a little confused. I remember asking my mum twice if she'd had breakfast yet. It was the following day, but I still thought it was the same morning of surgery. I thought it was pretty funny later. I asked for my phone to check the date and the medical staff were shocked that I remembered my pin after such a long surgery.

I was bed-bound and unable to walk after the surgery. It was only on the following morning that my mum realised that I could not move or do anything for myself. Everybody thought I could function because I talked and did not look too bad. I was getting bed baths and complete care from the nurses because I could not get out of bed. I was on heavy pain killers, morphine, to keep the pain away.

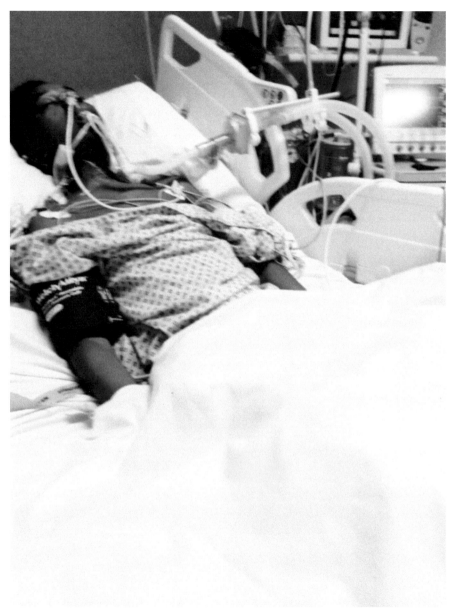

After second surgery, 19 September 2014

3

It wasn't over yet

The following day I remember being happy that I had made it through the surgery; it was all over. It hadn't registered then that I was bed-bound and couldn't walk. My mum came back in the morning with some family members, and it was then that the Consultants explained that it had been a highly complex surgery. They had not been able to remove the whole tumour because of where it had positioned itself in the brain. Attempting to remove all of it would have caused nerve damage, and as a result, they had only been able to remove 3 cm of the 5.5 cm tumour. They explained that they would have to operate the following day again, but after discussions in a Multidisciplinary Team Meeting (MDT), they agreed to wait because I was tired. So they decided to remove the rest of the tumour on the following Friday.

The doctors advised my mum that they would have to do the operation again. She was devasted and cried; she could not tell me and asked the doctors to tell me the news. When the doctors came to tell me, I refused to talk to them without my mum. I remember my heart dipping. I couldn't believe that I would have to go through the surgery again. After that, my mood switched, and I was so low and disappointed. I recall being overcome by feelings of sadness. The whole family was affected, and no one knew what to expect from the second surgery. I was dreading it, thinking it would be another fourteen hours in the theatre.

I was scared, and I remember posting a picture of my mum and myself on Facebook and Instagram, asking friends and family to pray for me. Many people responded, very concerned. They asked what was going on, but I could not respond to them because I was still not fully alert. Not many people knew that I had gone through major surgery and thought I had been in a car crash.

The fear was real

The days flew by; I was still bed-bound but able to eat. I was sleeping a lot because of the heavy painkillers, but I remember the fear growing and becoming very real as the days passed, getting closer to the second surgery date. I thought this time around, I would surely die. I tried hard not to show my fear because I did not want people to remember me as scared. I remained strong and positive in front of people, but honestly? Inside I was terrified.

Thanks, Marcus

I did have some positive thoughts, though, and my faith helped me immensely. For example, there is a video by Marcus Stanley (a famous pianist) that I watched all the time. It helped me when I had the first surgery, and I still listen to it now. It encourages and strengthens me. Marcus Stanley shares his amazing testimony with the world. He was shot eight times by gang members, and it is a miracle that he survived the shooting - his videos helped me fight the discouragement and depression and stay positive and believe that I would also make it through. I read that doctors performed an eight-hour surgery to save Marcus's life, removing half his stomach, reattaching his colon, half his pancreas and all his spleen. After the surgery, he sustained nerve damage in his arm, and his right hand had no feeling. He thought his musical career was over, but remarkably, after three months of rehab, he could walk again and even play the piano. Marcus's testimony keeps me going.

Here we go again

Friday soon came around, and it was time for the second surgery. I was again nil by mouth from midday to 8 am the following morning. This time around, I knew how major the operation was and this made me afraid. I was in the theatre for eight hours; the Surgeons didn't encounter as many complications as with the first surgery.

My mum came with my aunt and met with a Pastor in the car park who prayed for me and spoke over my life, that I would live and write a book. After that, other family members joined my mum and aunt, and they waited for me in the chapel, praying throughout the time that I was in the theatre.

After the surgery, I was taken to the Intensive Care Unit (ICU) and put on a breathing tube because I couldn't breathe independently. I was very poorly this time around and could not walk or swallow. I was basically unable to do anything. Everything around me was a blur, and I was on more painkillers than the last time. My memory was pretty rubbish; it had gone just like that.

My family, family friends and church family were all there for me throughout the whole experience. They visited, prayed and were very supportive. But unfortunately, the state I was in distressed them and most left the hospital in tears. My condition had deteriorated so much that I just lay, unmoving. Some people could not stay long because they could not hold back their tears and pain at seeing me in that state.

My thoughts and feelings during this time were all jumbled up. I remember having hallucinations, and I think this was because of the drugs. Eventually, I moved to the main ward for rehabilitation. I could not eat, walk, talk, or move independently, and my Consultants referred me for physio as well as Speech and Language therapy. Next, I transferred to a cancer specialist hospital for radiotherapy treatment, where I stayed for six weeks. Finally, after months in hospital, I made it back home in time for Christmas. It was my worst

Christmas ever because I was still recovering and adjusting to the new me; I did not feel the same.

I recall one of the highlights of my stay in the hospital was when Gary Cahill (ex-Chelsea Football player) and Jack Whitehall (Fulham football player) visited the Royal Marsden Hospital during my time there when I was receiving chemotherapy. I deferred starting university for a year to recover from the surgery. I don't think that I ever felt the same after that. Everything had changed.

With Gary Cahill, former Chelsea and England footballer

4

Life goes on…yet it was still not over yet!

A year later, I eventually went to University and started studying. It was a totally different world altogether, but I had a lot of support from the university and my cousins who attended the same university. Time passed, and when I got to my second year, the symptoms returned, more intense and challenging to my daily life. I experienced a whole cocktail of symptoms. I started to get double vision, headaches, intense dizziness and my balance was unsteady. I found the headaches to be more of an issue to deal with, and soon after, I started to get sick in the mornings. I was getting nausea, and it got awful. I kept going back to the GP, who would give me one prescription after another on each visit. I would be on one medication for a short time; for example, if I were prescribed antibiotics, I would take them for like seven days. If that didn't solve the issue - they would do more investigations and prescribe a different medication.

By this time, I could not keep up, let alone go to college; I was exhausted all the time. It was unusual for me because I'd always been an active sort of guy; I was happiest outside playing football. Soon my mood started to change because of the way I was feeling. Now it makes sense why my mood changed, but at the time, I was confused and didn't understand what was happening. Eventually, my mum began pre-packing meals to freeze, making my life easier.

My vision got worse, I couldn't see clearly; I began to fear going out independently. Initially, my mum thought I was a typical teenager, acting up but soon realised something was wrong.

After my second year at university, I had to go for a third operation. I was in surgery for eight hours, but this time around the after-effects were not as bad as the last two times. My main challenge following this surgery was experiencing weakness in my right shoulder; I could not lift anything heavy. Any movement on that side was very restricted. All the muscles on the right shoulder had decreased in size, and if I were to take my top off, you would see the difference between the two sides. I was getting a lot of pain from it. In addition, I had consistent ringing in the ears (tinnitus).

Radiotherapy treatment continued after this surgery, and I had to defer my studies for another year for recovery, therapy and rehabilitation. Whilst I was home recovering I started volunteering for Cancer charities like *Tindnights* to keep me busy. I enjoyed going out to these events because I connected with other people I could relate to regarding cancer. Before this, I hadn't connected with many people at all.

Life in the hospital

I've spent a lot of time in the hospital in the last few years and formed good relationships during my time there. I got on well with the doctors, nurses, and other patients on the wards. I was always friendly except when I was bed-bound and couldn't speak. The time I spent in ICU was the hardest; I wasn't 100% and couldn't focus on anything properly, but I could communicate by phone. I remember someone I made friends with within the same ward as me, and we were roughly the same age. We exchanged numbers and started talking through texts. We also exchanged social media account details. Upon reflection, it was rather courageous to step out like that and ask others to follow me on Social Media. When I was a bit better and able to walk and speak a little bit more, I made even more friends, and I am still friends with some of those people now.

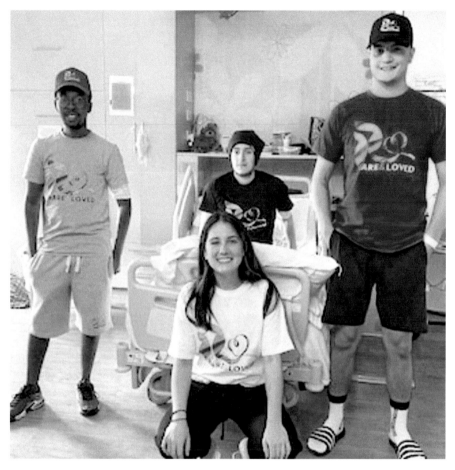

On the hospital ward with friends, wearing my Rare and Loved t-shirts

5

Starting all over again, learning to juggle life

After my year out, going back to university was like starting all over again, maybe even more challenging because my cousins were no longer there to support me. They had graduated, and my friends from the first and second years had graduated as well. So, I spent a lot of time in my room on my own. I had to make new friends; I didn't know any of the people in my dorm. I introduced myself to them and let them know what was up with me. I couldn't do much socialising in the first and second years because I struggled with my mental health. My new flatmates had no idea and thought that I was okay. I hadn't told them about my health issues; that would have taken too much time and effort.

I didn't go out much in fresher's week, choosing to stay in my room, unlike in years one and two when I did go out a bit, but it wasn't every day like most people. It was just a few times, but I felt the effects of going out till late more than everyone else in the mornings as I would suffer from extreme fatigue. University students go out a lot, and I missed out on socialising with other students because I couldn't go out much. I looked for other societies/activities that I could join e.g. where you could watch movies, play video games etc, but I couldn't find anything – so I was mostly in my room.

Too intense

The workload was heavy. I didn't expect it to be so intense because many people had told me that the third year is usually easier, so I went in believing for a much easier time. But from the word go it really was just go, and I did not go for my placement until much later down the line. In the first and second years, I used to go to the gym at least twice a week, which was on days that I did not have lectures. My cousin would pick me up and drive me there and back. I couldn't get to the gym on my own; it was a 20-minute walk that I couldn't make. It was only later that a friend who had a car would pick me up and take me there; it was the same with my placement. He would take me there and then come back for me. He did the same with some lectures because we were doing the same course. He was a great help because I was ridiculously exhausted most time.

It was hectic

Thursdays were hectic for me. I had lectures and seminars in the mornings and placement in the afternoon. It was a long day, and to cope, I would go to my room after the morning lectures and take a nap before going for the placements. I was studying Sports Therapy which was no joke. After the theory in class, we would have to put all we learned into practice. How did I survive? By taking long naps in between!

Socialising was a luxury that I could not afford. Between my busy schedule and the fatigue that gripped my body, I had no extra time; my life revolved around lectures, assignments and placement. And more assignments. My third year at Uni was the worst because it was so intense. I fell behind with a lot of my work. It sounds funny, but everything was assignment after assignment. I still had to keep up with regular check-ups and hospital appointments with all that going on. I never thought that I would struggle this much; the dissertation and the placements kept me busy. I had two placements, one at a Stroke Rehab centre and one at an Injury Sports Clinic. I needed to do the second placement because it was in line with my dissertation and would help keep the word count down. The work took its toll on my body, and I suffered.

It wasn't easy

I was very lonely. It was difficult having to start afresh after a year out. I hardly went out that last year. I had seven or eight flatmates, and there were two couples in the flat, a girl in a relationship whose boyfriend would visit. It felt awkward for me. They, of course, were okay with me, but it was hard for me to tell them my entire story so that they would understand why I acted a certain way. We were not close enough to have such deep conversations, maybe until later in the year. So, they only found out about my entire journey after graduation.

I only went out four times in that one year; making friends was hard because you only really meet people when you go out. I had to find ways to manage myself so that I would cope. I had to manage my days so that I could keep going. I needed a lot of rest time to recoup my energy levels after lectures. I suffered from depression and only accessed help later in the year. I had no one close to talk to about what I was going through. I'd had my cousins and my ex-girlfriend in my first and second years. Only when I accessed the counselling services at Uni, did I begin to cope better.

I worried and stressed about my weight. I had lost so much weight, and I didn't particularly appreciate how I looked. I always worried about my health and had constant appointments to keep up with. Even if I wanted to forget about my health, the symptoms would creep up to remind me. Unfortunately, I did not get to talk to anyone about it.

I couldn't have done it on my own

I struggled to keep up with the course/assignment deadlines, and most times,

I handed my work in late or after an extension was granted. Fortunately, the university assigned me a Study Skills Supporter for my three years there. She helped me to organise, plan and understand my work. Without this help, it would have been impossible for me to cope. In my last year, I had to work on my dissertation, and the other students had done a lot of work by April. I had not done much, and it was due at the end of May. It was a stressful time for me, and I had fallen behind on all my other work and didn't know how to manage it all. My Supervisor and the Study Skills Supporter helped even though I had to have two extensions which the Uni granted because they knew my circumstances.

My Social Worker, Liz, was there with me throughout my journey and had been so since 2014. She would come to Uni to meet up with me, and we would talk. Her help made such a difference. She had been there from the beginning and seen me through all the different treatments. She had seen me complete the first year, complete the second year, and have that third surgery and radiotherapy. And, she saw me through graduation day. She had seen me through it all and motivated and encouraged me all the way. She was amazing and always listened when I needed to talk. Thank you, Liz!

6

My life will never be the same

Post-Op effects on my health

My life has changed forever. After the operations and treatments, some of my body's movements have become restricted, e.g. lifting my right arm. This is because to get to the tumour, the surgeons had to touch the 10th cranial nerve, which controls the right shoulder and affects movement on that side of my shoulders.

My right leg is now weak. After the third surgery, I remember I could not lift my right leg for three days. Since then, I get the occasional pain; if I get a cold, flu or strong headache, I get pain in my right leg. My voice was affected massively after the first surgery. The right vocal cord hasn't worked correctly since then. After the surgery, my voice was low, and all I could do at the time was a whisper, and I had trouble swallowing. The muscles in my throat were not working correctly. Up to today, I cannot raise my voice or shout.

After the treatments, I got tinnitus—a constant ringing in my ears since 2015. I have it in both ears now following the most recent surgery. I live with the ringing every day, and I've had to get used to it. The muscles in my right shoulder are now rounded; they have reduced and weakened. I am right-handed, but I have learned to compensate with the left side after the treatments and operations. The vision in my right eye got worse. If I look to the right with my right eye, involuntarily it goes back to the middle.

Mental Health is real

My community does not talk much about mental health issues, almost as if it's non-existent. I didn't know much about Mental health, even when I struggled with it. Because of all the things happening to me, I found myself in a dark place. In my free time and at night, on my own, I would find myself in deep thoughts. It wasn't very nice, and I did not have anyone to confide in. I suffered from depression without knowing what it was. I was sad all the time and kept away from people. I had many insecurities due to the surgeries that I had undergone and was very self-conscious about my voice and how I walked.

I managed a bit better in my first and second years than in my third year. As I said, I never really understood what mental health was back then. I would hear people say that they were depressed but did not understand it. I never thought that I suffered from depression and told myself that I was okay and hadn't been depressed yet; I believed my mental health was good. After I attended some workshops with different charities that addressed mental health issues, I then knew more about what I was going through in the third year. Healing from a brain injury takes a long time; it is very slow. My mental health was affected, and I wanted to hide from the world

Tupac Music – My escape

Listening to music helped me to cope. I loved listening to Tupac because I felt I could relate to the struggles that he addressed in his music. His music became my go-to escape. I've always been a Tupac fan since before the diagnosis. I could relate to it. He rapped a lot about the struggle. He also mentions his mum's struggles as a single mum. I could connect. There was a time that I listened to him every day; I would put my earphones in and listen and escape.

I had hundreds of his songs on my phone, but the ones I mostly kept going back to were:

- *To live and die in LA*
- *Life goes on*
- *Hit him up*
- *Dear mama*
- *Changes*
- *Letter to my unborn child*

7

My Timeline

I remember having so many anxieties and being confused because I had no idea what was going on. I was a healthy, active, fit teenager without any worries. I spent time outside playing football with my friends. Then the diagnosis came, and it affected my mental health; I was stressed all the time, worrying about my health. Physically I began to grow weaker, and we noticed that my right eyelid would droop, mostly when I was tired. Fatigue was a big thing. I was always tired.

I honestly think the diagnosis also impacted and interrupted my puberty. I seem to have stopped growing because I believe I should be taller than I am. So I started puberty late, and soon after that, I got the diagnosis, but I had been feeling the symptoms for two years before that.

I remember feeling so sad all the time.

< **Timeline** 📖 🖇 ⋮

•Diagnosed Grade II Ependymoma September 4th 2014.
• 1st surgery 12th September 2014
• 2nd surgery 19th September 2014
• 33 sessions of radiotherapy completed 15th January 2015
• 1st year university September 2015
• 2nd year university - September 2016
• 3rd surgery- 10th August 2017
• 30 sessions of radiotherapy - completed 7th November 2017
• 3rd year university - September 2018
• Graduated- July 2019

8

My 'go-to' inspiration

I would be lying if I said that my journey has been easy because it hasn't. I found myself wanting to give up so many times. I recall that once going into the hospital, putting my little sister's fingerprint to unlock my phone so that if something happened during surgery, she would access information on my phone. I had to find some encouragement to keep fighting, and I found this in a few inspirational people that I follow. I watched videos and listened to their stories and was encouraged to keep fighting:

Anthony Burns - Anthony is a young motivational speaker who has faced many personal challenges, and his inspiration and motivation to change lives are derived from these personal experiences. He *says, "The one thing that should keep you motivated with energy and drive is the fact that you still have life... .The biggest thing I leant was to never give up, no matter the situation... Big or Small."* He inspired me with his motivational videos. I had started watching him before the surgeries and have continued to do so to date.

Tyler Perry – Tyler is a black American actor, writer and producer. In 2011, he was listed as the highest-paid man in entertainment, earning US$130 million. (Wikipedia). I love his motivational videos on Youtube, which inspire and motivate me. When he acquired his latest studios, he spoke about the final push I needed to start my own business, "Rare and Loved". He says if you are black, you have to work harder to achieve your dreams.

Steve Harvey - Broderick Stephen Harvey born January 17, 1957, is an American comedian, businessman and entertainer. He hosts The Steve Harvey Show, Family Feud, Celebrity Family Feud, the Miss Universe competition, since 2015, and Fox's New Year's Eve, since 2017.[1] Steve went from being homeless with $35 in his wallet to become an acclaimed media personality worth millions.

Inky Johnson - Inquoris "Inky" Johnson is an American motivational speaker and former college football player. His football career ended in 2006 at the University of Tennessee with an injury that permanently paralysed his right arm. [2]

Eric Thomas - *I firmly believe if you don't know you can fly, you'll always think you can't.* Eric Thomas is an author, preacher and motivational speaker, who has inspired and impacted many lives. His motivational speeches and videos have also kept me going.

My Faith, My belief

I believe in God. I am a Christian, and my faith helped me stay positive during my journey. It helped me to have hope. My faith in God remained strong, and there is not a day that I questioned God, *WHY ME?* I would never wish what I had gone through on anyone else. Instead, my fight against brain cancer has strengthened over the years. I would say that my relationship with God has improved. Before the diagnosis, I used to play the piano, but I felt forced to do so. Now, I love to play, I love to worship, and my prayer life is a lot more improved. I have grown spiritually, and I have two scriptures that I held on to, still do, that kept me going:

Roman 8:18 - *For I consider that the sufferings of this present time are not worthy to be compared with the glory which shall be revealed in us. (NKJV)*

Jeremiah 29:11 - *For I know the thoughts that I think toward you, says the Lord, thoughts of peace and not of evil, to give you a future and a hope. (NKJV)*

9

Graduation Finally! – It felt good

Before graduation day came, it hadn't quite sunk in that I was finally done with University. On the day, everyone wished me well and congratulated me, which made it start to sink in; I was graduating; I had done it! IT ALL SUNK IN when I finally had the gown on, the hat, and walked on stage. Yes! I had finally made it! After years of juggling the lectures, assignments, placement, the symptoms, treatments, and endless appointments that I had to endure, it was such a great feeling. It was one of the best and most memorable days of my life, and I thoroughly loved and enjoyed the day.

I held on and did not give up because I thought people would think I was a failure. I thought the same for myself, and I kept pushing myself, telling myself that I was almost there; *Tawanda, you are almost finished; you are almost graduating.* I was very very close to giving up multiple times. I appreciate that I was fortunate enough to have a lot of help, encouragement and cheerleaders who kept me going; my family, my surgeon and my Social Worker. And the support and understanding that I got from the University were invaluable.

Thank you all!

Graduation, 2019

10

Brain Tumour 101: A Few Facts

When I was first diagnosed, I knew nothing about cancers, let alone ependymomas. However, soon after that diagnosis, I began finding out more about this sickness attacking my body. Below are some definitions and facts that became common knowledge to me as I journeyed and fought for my life. It may help you to understand what I went through.

What is a brain tumour?

A brain tumour is a growth in your brain. It can be non-cancerous (benign) or cancerous (malignant). Brain tumours are classified as either benign or malignant. The benign ones tend to grow more slowly and are less likely to come back if they've been completely removed. The malignant ones tend to grow faster, sometimes spread, and come back after treatment. They're both treated in similar ways – but the exact care you receive depends on what type of tumour you have, where it is in the brain and how big it is. [3]

What is Ependymoma

An ependymoma is a rare type of brain tumour that develops from the ependymal cells that line the passageways containing cerebral spinal fluid.

30

Therefore, they are found in the walls of the ventricles or the spinal cord central canal. Ependymoma can be found in any part of the brain or spine, but in children, they are more common in the cerebellum, in the posterior fossa, a small space located at the back of the brain near the brain stem. Ependymomas represent approximately 1.9% of all primary brain and central nervous system tumours and around 25% of spinal tumours. Ependymomas can also form in the choroid plexus. [4]

What causes Ependymoma

Ependymomas develop from ependymal cells, which are a type of glial cell. Glial cells provide the structure around neural cells within the brain and help to keep the neural cells healthy. However, when the DNA within an ependymal cell becomes damaged, it can replicate itself uncontrolled without apoptosis.[5] This uncontrolled growth is what leads to the formation of a tumour.

Common Symptoms:

- Headaches
- Feeling or being sick
- Problems with coordination and balance
- Problems with sight
- Seizures (Fits)
- Being confused
- Changes in mood and personality, but this is rare.

Treating Ependymoma

There are different ways of treating Ependymoma:

Neurosurgery

Surgery to remove as much of the tumour as possible is the first line of treatment for ependymomas. After surgery, the doctor will create a treatment plan.

Radiotherapy

Radiotherapy uses controlled doses of high-energy radiation beams to destroy tumour cells whilst causing as little damage as possible to surrounding cells.

Chemotherapy

Chemotherapy involves taking drugs that have been developed to kill tumour cells. They are either taken as a pill or using an injection or drip.

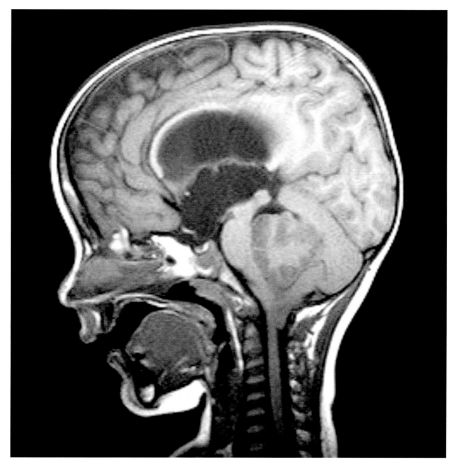

Brain Tumour Image [3]

11

Support that could help

Tere's so much support out there now than was available a few years back. For anyone going through this same journey, I encourage you to connect with other people you can relate to, people who can help you and support you. The truth is that it's not going to be easy, and that is the absolute truth. There will be good days and very bad days, but don't determine your whole life based on a few bad days. So, I just want to say, hang in there and stay strong. Things will get better.

The best way to "hang in there" is to:

- Watch motivational videos (I watched a lot of these).
- Try to think positively, to think and push past the pain.
- Life could be a lot worse. The fact that you still have life in you means that you still have a purpose. Appreciate the life that you have.
- Speak. Talk to someone. Don't keep things in because they pile up, and that's not healthy.
- Find support in the community, i.e. Charities e.t.c
- Pray if you can. Have faith.

The support that would have been the most helpful for me:

Family and friends. I wish they could have better understood what I was going through; that would have helped me mentally. Some thought I was okay when I wasn't because I would answer that I was okay whenever they asked me how I was. But if they spent time with me, talking with me, I would feel free enough to explain what was going on in my life. It's hard to tell people just upfront that your mental health is struggling. Prayer is good, but sometimes you need to talk to someone.

Community - I wish I had met more people like myself in the community or the charities that I reached out to. In the early days, it was hard, but later, I met some members of the black community going through the same health challenges who were willing to talk about their journeys. It helps when the community knows how to support and help someone with a life-changing diagnosis. My family, as my carers, also need support to deal with their emotions and exhausting caring responsibilities.

Charities - There weren't many people from my community accessing the services from the charities that offered support to brain cancer patients. It was and still is challenging to find someone who understands Black Minority Ethnicity (BME) issues in these charities. It was hard to relate even to the staff. It would make such a difference in BME's lives if the Charities and caregivers understand the different cultural backgrounds and beliefs. This way, they would offer a more holistic approach.

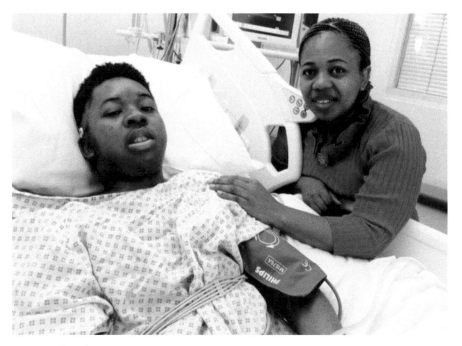

After first surgery, King's College Hospital, 12 September 2014

12

Rare and Loved – Giving back

Rare and Loved is a Social Enterprise that I started in 2020 to raise awareness of brain cancer and its effects on patients and their families, especially in the BME (Black Minority Ethnic) communities. For years I wanted to start something of my own, and what finally pushed me to start was mainly my mum and the inspiration I got from Tyler Perry. My mum always encouraged me to start my own business; she has no idea how much her words and encouragement had on me.

The messages by Tyler Perry pushed me to start, especially when he acquired his latest studio. He said that you are not invited to where they are at; create your own platform, which he did. I've had a few rejections from Charities I felt should have given me some support, and I have felt let down by them.

The reason behind the Rare and Loved brand is to give back to the community which I believe will help others going through hardships, cancer, or any other rare medical conditions. There is so much that could have helped and supported me through the worst parts of my journey, which was not available to me, this is what I want to give to others.

Rare and Loved is for extraordinary individuals who have a health condition or a life experience that sets them apart. It is a home and platform for fighters who are RARE and LOVED! We give support by providing:

- information,
- inspiration,
- support groups,
- a listening ear and
- online networking opportunities.

We are a safe place to meet others going through the same challenges, a place to be accepted and not judged. We are also suppliers of fashionable, branded clothing merchandise for everyday use.

Modeling Rare and Loved apparel 2021

13

Tawanda Forever

The tumours came back in 2018

What happens with the Epyndemomas is that they spread into other areas of the body if they do come back. When they came back in 2018, they were detected in the brain and my spine. It is unclear how much of them are in my body because they run in the fluid, and it is hard to detect the smaller tumours. They came back as a grade III tumour. It is now an anaplastic brain tumour (brain and spine).

I have been on two different oral chemotherapy treatments from October to November 2019. I took the tablets for three days and then had four weeks of rest. After the rest, I would retake them for another three days. I did that for a short while until the doctors realised that the treatment wasn't working. The tumours were continuing to grow.

They put me on a different treatment, and I did three cycles of the new treatment, which worked for a little while. The problem was that the treatment only worked on some tumours and not others, the brain tumours were stable, but the ones in the spine continued to grow. So, the doctors decided that I needed a stronger treatment that would target all of the tumours at once. But because of the lockdown, I had to wait before going on the new treatment. I was reluctant and scared about going on this treatment. I did not want to have stronger treatment.

I began the new treatment in July 2020. This treatment initially involved four different kinds of chemotherapies which I would have at different times. Treatment one was for three days, two nights and one day. I would have twenty-two days of rest before the next treatment. I did this cycle, and I got many infections when I was in the treatment. I was in the hospital a lot after the treatments because of how they affected my body.

After the first treatment, I had side effects. I had tinnitus. My hands and feet went numb, and I experienced some tingling in my hands and feet. I felt tired and weak. The doctors decided to lower one of the doses, which caused the tingling, but I still got the other side effects. So eventually, they took that treatment off because it lowered my quality of life.

My sodium levels dropped significantly. A normal reading is 130, but mine dropped to 105 very quickly, which was quite dangerous. The drug that caused this also increased the tinnitus, and they took it off and gave me something similar. I have now done five treatments. I have a few more to go, and then I am finished with it. After I complete this round, they say that they will decide whether I need more or whether it worked well enough to take me off.

I've been a lot stronger this time around with all these treatments. The first MRI scan was positive because the tumours had shrunk compared with the MRI scan from two months ago. My next scan is at the beginning of November 2020, and I feel optimistic about it. I believe the results will be a lot more positive.

Life

I am at home, taking it easy because of the treatments and side effects and because of COVID, I don't go out. If I am not home, I am at the hospital. I do not go to other people's houses because I am shielding. If I have enough energy, I work on Rare and Loved or talk to friends on the phone. I also educate and develop myself and have done a few business courses in the last two months. I go on ZOOM meetings with Charities and participate in their activities. I have done some work with the Princess Trust.

The Future

In the past, I made plans, but my health disrupted every plan I had; I have not been able to do much. I am not sure if I will ever use my degree in the future. I think I will do more stuff with Rare and Loved. I see the brand and business growing. I see myself working at my own pace without pressure from others, and I love it because it is something that I created from scratch.

Travelling

I love travelling, and I see myself travelling more and even living in another country. I have travelled to nine countries so far. My plan this year was to visit South Africa for three months, but because of Covid and my health complications, that plan did not happen.

Family

I would love to have a wife and family. So I look forward to that a lot and believe that I will have my own family and be very happy.

My thoughts concerning this journey

"What if" has been my main question. What I have thought about is: yes - I have had all these *"what-if"* questions, but I have come to the realisation that my life is different from most. The doctors have said that my case has been different from the beginning, and I believe that miracles still happen. I have good thoughts about my future. I want to bring awareness, and making people aware of brain cancer makes me feel better. So many people are ignorant about this diagnosis, and one of my coping mechanisms and go-to's is letting people know through Social Media. I use Facebook, Instagram and Twitter to talk about my journey and inform people about brain cancers. I get excited when I get responses; it makes me feel better. A lot of people need education on being cancer survivors. One of the challenges I have is that my speaking and writing abilities got affected by the tumours and treatments. I would love to write and speak more. I am dyslexic, so the struggle is real, especially after the surgeries.

With *family 2021*

14

I have dreams

The dreams that I've had have changed over the past few years.

When I was younger, I dreamt of being rich and having all these luxurious things. But now all this has changed. I have learnt that those things will not give me true happiness. I want a happy family, I want my own family and I want my family to be comfortable.

I want to leave a legacy so that people will remember me for what I will have done. I want to help people with cancer, people with brain tumours. People going through tough times as I did. I know that I have a lot to give, I have a big heart.

I would like to make my mum and little sister happy. I want to get them the things they need just to make them more comfortable and I know that I will get to that point where I will be able to do this for them. My sister was very young when I was diagnosed and she didn't understand much of what was going on but I know that my journey has had a huge impact on her life. I feel that I need to do something really nice for her.

And my mum...

I know she is my mum and is meant to be by my side but it's been a lot for her. I want to buy them stuff; a house, a car.....I want to make them happy...

Tawanda Forever

Red carpet moments 2021

15

April 2021: I rang the bell!

T oday I rang the bell! Cancer patients ring the bell to signify the end of treatment. It felt good to ring the bell and I spent the whole day smiling. I could not believe that I had completed the chemotherapy treatment.

Ringing the bell, after completing chemotherapy

Brain Cancer Support

Teenage Cancer Trust

The Trust creates world-class cancer services for young people in the UK, providing life-changing care and support so young people don't have to face cancer alone.

https://www.teenagecancertrust.org/

The Brain Tumour Charity

The Brain Tumour Charity is the world's leading brain tumour charity and the largest dedicated funder of research into brain tumours globally.

https://www.thebraintumourcharity.org/

Notes

MY 'GO-TO' INSPIRATION

1   Wikipedia

2   Wikipedia

BRAIN TUMOUR 101: A FEW FACTS

3   Teenagecancertrust.org

4   https://www.braintumourresearch.org/info-support/resources/glossary-of-terms

5   https://www.braintumourresearch.org/info-support/resources/glossary-of-terms